HOW THEY LIVED

A CRUSADING KNIGHT

STEWART ROSS

Illustrated by
Mark Bergin

ROURKE ENTERPRISES, INC.
Vero Beach, Florida 32964

First published in the
United States in 1987 by
Rourke Enterprises, Inc.
PO Box 3328, Vero Beach,
Florida 32964

First published in 1986 by
Wayland (Publishers) Limited
61 Western Road, Hove
East Sussex BN3 1JD, England

Library of Congress Cataloging-in-Publication Data

Ross, Stewart.
A crusading knight.

(How they lived)
Bibliography: p.
Includes index.
Summary: Describes the background of the Crusades and
the day-to-day life of knights who pledged to fight in
them. Also discusses the weapons, methods of warfare,
and final outcome of these campaigns.
1. Crusades—Juvenile literature.   2. Knights and
knighthood—Europe—Juvenile literature.   [1. Crusades.
2. Knights and knighthood]   I. Bergin, Mark, ill.
II. Title.   III. Series.
D160.R67 1986   909.07   86–20263

ISBN 0–86592–142–3

Typeset by Kalligraphics Ltd, Redhill, Surrey
Printed in Italy by G. Canale & C.S.p.A., Turin

CONTENTS

TAKING THE CROSS

The sun shone brightly through the stained-glass church window, and fell on a young soldier kneeling in prayer. He had been there all night. It was morning now, and time for him to take his vow.

The man was a crusader. He was about to leave home and travel many miles to fight for Christianity. Perhaps he would never return. The church door opened and the priest entered to hear the knight's promise. It was too late to turn back now.

Since the first century A.D., Christians had visited the towns of Bethlehem and Jerusalem. In 1071, however, fierce Muslim Turks, called Saracens, seized control of these shrines. This made Christian pilgrimages impossible. So, in 1095, Pope Urban II called for the Christians of western Europe to drive the Saracens from the Holy Land. Soldiers who volunteered wore red crosses on their clothes and were called "crusaders."

The young soldier in the church was one of thousands who took the cross and vowed to recapture the Holy Land. One of their aims was to free the Church of the Holy Sepulcher in Jerusalem. This church was especially important to Christians as it was said to have been built on the site of Jesus' tomb.

Their task was very difficult. The first crusaders set out in 1096. There were eight crusades in all, taking place over a period of 195 years. Yet when the last crusaders left the Holy Land in 1291, the Holy Places had once again fallen into Muslim hands.

CHRISTIAN TERRITORY
MUSLIM TERRITORY

The map shows the different areas controlled by Christians and Muslims at the time of the first crusade.

WHY THEY WENT

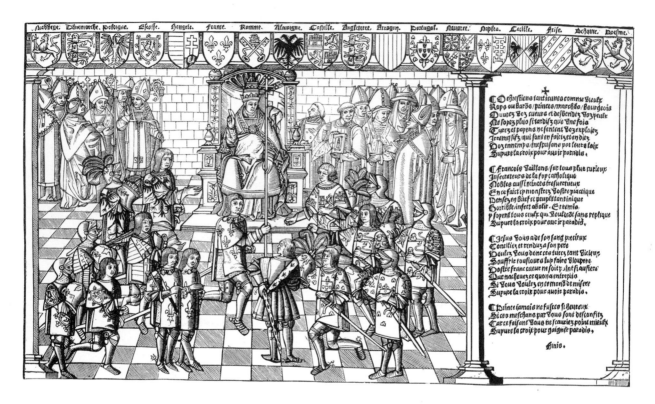

Medieval knights had a strong sense of duty. When Pope Urban summoned them "to drive out the Turk," they knew they should obey. He went on to remind crusaders what a beautiful thing it would be to die in Jerusalem, where Christ had died.

Stories were spread about the Saracens which made them seem like devils. Rumors said they collected the skulls of their victims, and

Pope Urban II calling Christians to join the first crusade. The 16th-century poem describes the crusaders' journey to Jerusalem.

enjoyed torturing their enemies. The knights burned with anger and longed for revenge when they heard these tales. Some sold all their possessions to pay for their crusade. Those who did not go were called cowards.

6

Saracens looting a Christian city.

There were other reasons why a knight went on crusade. The pope said that crusaders would be forgiven their past sins, so men took the cross to show repentance for evil deeds. Others went in search of riches. The cities of the east were famous for their wealth: in 1204, soldiers of the fourth crusade did not even reach the Holy Land. They plundered the Christian city of Byzantium instead.

Some knights hoped to conquer land for themselves; some sought glory; others became crusaders for adventure, or just because they liked fighting. A crusade was a holy war, but the reasons why knights fought were not always very religious.

Turkish troops marching away from a city with their baggage wagons.

7

LIFE AT HOME

Crusading knights came from western Europe. Life then was much simpler than today. Most people were poor farmers, living in tiny cottages in villages. There were few towns and very little trade. Science was scarcely understood, so there was no electricity or gas, no cars, airplanes, running water or sewers. Knowledge of medicine was slight and epidemics of dreadful diseases swept the countryside. Famine was common.

Government was in the hands of the king. He had no police to help him, and the law courts were often unfair. Life was tough. Fights and small wars continually broke out. Those who could afford to, built themselves castles for protection.

Soldiers were of great importance in this warlike society. A knight was a professional soldier and his job was to protect his lord. In return for an oath of loyalty, the lord gave the knight land. The knight had to live on the income from this land.

All the people in this society were part of a feudal system, which was based on the amount of the land you held. The great lords held their land directly from the king, and they swore oaths to him. Ordinary people,

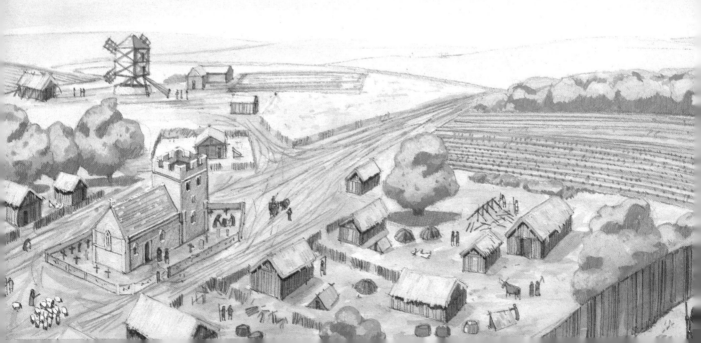

called villeins, held no land. They had to work for their lord, and get his permission for almost everything they did. They were near the bottom of the feudal system. The knight, however, was at its heart.

Above *A knight kneels before his lord and swears an oath of loyalty to him.*

THE CHURCH AND CHIVALRY

At the time of the crusades religion played a much larger part in people's lives than it does today. In western Europe everyone belonged to the Roman Catholic Church, which had the pope at its head. Some popes claimed to be more important and powerful than kings and emperors.

The Church owned a great deal of land in all European countries. This made it very wealthy. It also controlled the schools and universities where knights were educated. So, from their earliest days, knight were taught to honor and protect the Christian Church. They went to church very often, spending at least an hour each day in prayer.

Crusading knights were supposed to be ideal Christian gentlemen. They followed a code of behavior called chivalry. This said that they were to be kind and generous to the weak, but hard yet just on the wicked. At all times they were to be honest, fair and modest.

Young boys practicing tilting, a form of jousting, on a wooden horse.

In the summer, mock battles, called tournaments, were held in front of large crowds. Knights on horseback fought each other with long lances. This was known as jousting. Such tournaments were only practice fights. The knights who left on crusade longed to test their skills in real battle against the enemies of the Church.

A medieval tournament.

WEAPONS AND ARMOR

Knights were the most powerful part of a crusading army. Each knight wore woolen underwear, and a heavy leather jerkin. On his legs he had thick stockings, over which he pulled chain mail leg pieces. These were made of hundreds of little steel rings looped together. To his heels the knight strapped spurs.

A chain mail coat, called a hauberk, covered the knight's body to his knees. On his head he wore a kind of balaclava helmet which was also made of mail. Armored gloves protected his hands.

By the third crusade knights wore massive steel helmets. Some just had a lengthened nose piece for protection, while others covered the whole

Knights were helped into battle dress by their servants.

face and neck. Such helmets were so hot and heavy they could only be worn for about two hours at a time. Over their armor crusaders wore loose white coats. These helped to keep them cool by reflecting the sun.

Knights were armed with lances for charging, which were often over 10 feet (3 meters) long. For hand-to-hand fighting they carried huge swords and daggers. Their thick shields were triangular, and made of wood and leather. A knight in full armor was quite safe from attack, but he was slow and clumsy. His horse had to be very strong, too, for a knight's armor and weapons could weigh as much as 100 pounds (45 kilograms).

A knight's full armor was heavy and awkward.

Below are some examples of a knight's armor and weaponry.

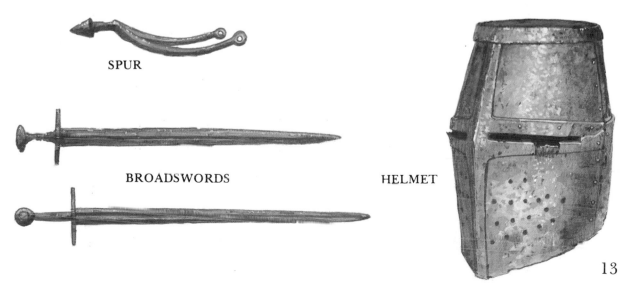

SPUR

BROADSWORDS

HELMET

13

THE JOURNEY TO THE HOLY LAND

The knight we met on page 4 did not go on crusade alone. He was one of several knights who traveled with their lord, together with numerous foot soldiers and servants. In 1190 all these bands joined together with the army of King Richard I – Richard the Lionheart, the most famous crusader of all.

Crusaders could travel to Palestine overland or by sea; neither journey was easy. When Richard set out, the Emperor Barbarossa of Germany also left for the Holy Land with an army.

Barbarossa's army took the long, dangerous overland route. Many soldiers were killed when their horses stumbled on narrow mountain paths.

The Emperor himself drowned while crossing a river. In Asia, his army was ambushed by fierce Muslim bands, and food became so scarce that the knights had to eat their horses. Many returned home. Out of the 300,000 men who set out, only 2,000 reached the Holy Land.

Richard's army traveled by sea. One knight wrote that he was terrified of "the roar of the crashing waves, and the ships creaking in the mighty wind." Ships were not very safe in those days and some men were shipwrecked.

This painting shows knights getting ready to sail for the Holy Land.

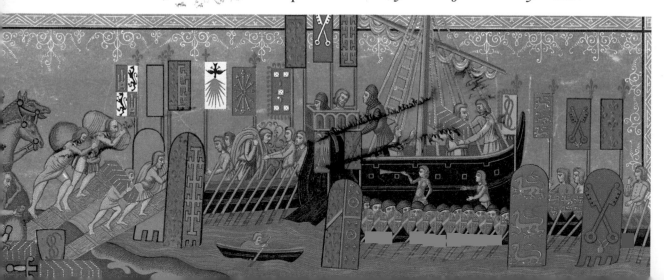

Many crusaders lost their lives on the journey across the Mediterranean.

IN CAMP

Crusading knights were not always marching and fighting. A good deal of their time was spent in camp. Knights went on crusade dreaming of glory and great victories. Weeks spent in camp, waiting for the leaders to decide what to do, were dull and disappointing.

In camp a knight lived in a large, bright tent. His servants were responsible for putting this up, and seeing that their master was well looked after. His clothes, weapons and armor were cleaned and repaired, and his horses groomed.

The knight, if he was a religious man, prayed regularly each day on crusade. There were always plenty of priests to celebrate mass. If a battle or a march was about to start, the knight rested. Otherwise he spent his day amusing himself as best he could, and talking to other knights, trying to find out what their next move would be.

This picture shows a crusaders' camp. The knights' tents were placed in the center of the camp, with the soldiers and servants around them.

The heat and the flies were terrible. Knights soon grew bored and angry. Fights often broke out, and men were killed. Sensible leaders organized tournaments to keep the warlike knights occupied. Sometimes, however, there were full-scale

Waiting in camp made the knights restless and fights were common.

battles between different groups of crusaders. When this happened, knights wondered why they had bothered to come on the crusade.

17

FOOD AND DRINK

Crusading armies were not well organized. Knights often found it difficult to get the food and drink they needed. The biggest problem in the Holy Land was getting fresh water.

Palestine is a dry country. At the time of the crusades drinking water was usually drawn from wells, which could be filled in or poisoned by the enemy. During the first crusade knight sewed ox skins together to

In temperatures of 100°F (38°C) the knights grew very thirsty.

In between battles, knights would enjoy good food and wine.

make water carriers. The water tasted revolting. At the battle of Hattin, during the second crusade, the knights of King Guy were so hot and thirsty that they just lay on the ground, unable to fight.

Knights on crusade liked to drink wine, but they found the heavy eastern wines strange at first. The food was unusual too. Sugar, not honey, was used to sweeten food. Exotic spices, such as nutmeg and cinnamon, helped to preserve food in the hot climate.

For a typical meal the knight had roasted meat – perhaps from a camel – and thick bread. Melons and other fruit lay on the table, while red wine filled his goblet. On the march, however, he was lucky to get dirty water and a handful of raisins.

19

HEALTH

Far more crusading knights died of disease than were killed by the Saracens. The most common illnesses were caused by dirty food and drink, which caused sickness and diarrhea. Frequently the victims died.

Sometimes knights were bitten by

A medieval surgeon, in his everyday clothes, treating an eye injury.

Battle wounds were not kept clean and often became infected.

snakes or poisonous spiders. Injury in battle was a more serious danger. In hot weather wounds quickly became infected. Medieval doctors did not understand how important it was to keep wounds clean. Sometimes they put dung on them. As a result, damaged limbs often had to be cut off. This was done without anesthetic and many patients died of

20

shock or infection. Even if a knight survived the operation, he was no longer useful as a crusader. He had to make his own way home as best he could.

The health of knights was not always poor. If they survived the journey to Palestine, and if they were not wounded, they lived well. The climate was pleasant, and they enjoyed the luxuries of the east.

Many knights settled in Palestine after the first crusade, and some began to wear Saracen clothes. Pilgrims arriving from Europe were shocked; they saw these knights as traitors.

Medical treatment was very basic and strange ointments were mixed for treating wounds. One was made of crushed worms and lice.

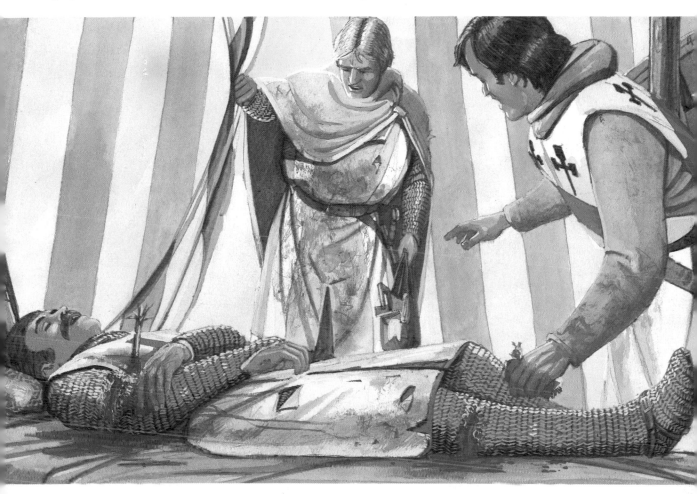

SIEGE

Knights fought best on horseback in open battle, but much of their time in the Holy Land was spent in sieges. The knights of the first crusade besieged the city of Antioch for seven months before it fell. The fortress of Acre held out against the soldiers of the third crusade for two years.

When a castle or city was besieged, the knights saved themselves for the hand-to-hand fighting. At first ordinary foot soldiers and engineers tried to batter down the walls and gates with fire, machines, and mines. Then, when the signal was given, the attack began.

Some knights climbed ladders put up against the walls. Others went up huge siege towers and across wooden bridges into the castle. As they made their attack the Saracens bombarded them with all kinds of missiles. They threw boiling tar and jars full of poisonous snakes at them. Arrows, spears and stones also rained down on the attacking soldiers.

The worst weapon of the Saracens was "Greek Fire." This was a mixture of gasoline and tar. The defenders set it on fire and sprayed it onto attacking knights. The flames went underneath their armor and caused horrible burns. The crusaders soon learned to use "Greek Fire" themselves when they were defending their own castles.

While soldiers weaken the castle wall and the siege tower is put in position, the enemy retaliates with "Greek Fire." The crossbowman provides covering fire for the besiegers.

BATTLE

At Arsuf on September 7, 1191, the army of Richard I met that of the great Saracen leader, Saladin, in one of the biggest battles of the crusades. Never did the Christian knights fight so well.

Richard's army was marching to Jerusalem when it was ambushed. The crusaders were suddenly attacked by 10,000 mounted Turks. Richard ordered his knights not to charge. Instead, soldiers with bows and arrows broke up the Muslim attack. Then, when the enemy were disorganized, six trumpets sounded. It was the signal for the knights to attack.

The sight and sound of hundreds of charging knights was terrifying.

Hooves thundered on the dry desert and a vast cloud of dust rose into the air. Gradually, the huge horses gathered speed. The knights lowered their long lances, aiming at the Turkish ranks. Then, with a crash, the two armies met.

The force of the knights' charge was enormous. The Turks were pushed back, many pierced by lances. Now the knights drew their swords or axes and started hacking at the shaken enemy. Before long, the Turks were fleeing for their lives, leaving thousands of their men dead behind them. Saladin learned that it was unwise to face crusader knights in open battle.

Saladin lost almost 7,000 men at Arsuf, while Richard lost around 700 men.

AT EASE

After a hard fight crusading knights needed to relax. They enjoyed huge feasts with plenty to drink. While minstrels sang songs about heroic deeds of chivalry, servants brought in delicious food and jugs of wine.

In quieter moments knights might relax by playing dice or chess, a game they learned from the Arabs. Some took an interest in Arabs learning, which was more advanced than that of the west. Those who settled in Palestine found it useful to learn Arabic. The numbers we use today come from the Arabs. They replaced the more awkward Roman numerals.

Energetic knights took part in tournaments. These were even more magnificent than those arranged at home. Beautiful oriental silks and carpets decorated the stands where the audience sat. The knights wore colorful coats embroidered with gold

A game of chess between a crusader and a Saracen.

Above *Medieval musicians, known as minstrels, provided entertainment for the knights.*

Silver candlesticks brought home from the crusades.

and silver thread. Stories of such eastern splendor spread back to Europe, encouraging more crusaders to volunteer.

Knights who had been victorious in war spent much of their leisure time collecting treasures to take home. They gathered luxurious robes of purple and scarlet, silk cloaks, silver candlesticks and dishes, carpets, cushions, casks and sacks of exotic spices. Crusading was a dangerous undertaking. But a knight who did survive enjoyed a better life than he had before.

THE JOURNEY HOME

Many knights took the overland journey home, rather than travel by sea.

After the first and third crusades some knights remained in the Holy Land to look after their estates. Others joined one of the new orders (groups) of knights founded during the crusades. These were the Templar Knights (who guarded the Holy Places) and the Knights of St. John. When the fighting was over, however, most surviving soldiers left for home.

Returning knights loaded their possessions onto wagons, hired guards, and joined with others making the same journey. Some went by sea but many, like King Richard, traveled home overland.

The journey back was usually easier than the passage to the Holy Land had been. Knights knew what they had to expect, and were hardened and experienced soldiers now. Brigands who attacked returning crusaders were either very brave or very foolish.

A crusader knight who returned was a respected member of the community. Friends and family wondered at the treasures he brought with him, and in the long winter evenings they listened eagerly to his tales of the shame and glory of the crusades.

Among his treasures, the returned crusader displays some of the Arabs' skillful craftwork.

THE END OF THE CRUSADES

Knights were never more important than at the time of the crusades. In the fourteenth century the English discovered that arrows fired from longbows could destroy a charge of mounted knights. Soon afterwards gunpowder was discovered, and armored knights became obsolete.

In the end, the crusaders failed to recapture the Holy Land. Yet their efforts had not been wasted. Europeans learned much from the Arabs, about fortifications, medicine, mathematics and other branches of knowledge. They were introduced to new goods, such as cotton, and new foods. Perhaps the crusading knights were more important for what they brought home than for all their brave struggles to conquer the Holy Land.

From eastern castles such as this one, crusaders learned much about improving the building of their castles at home.

GLOSSARY

Anesthetic Something that puts a person to sleep during surgery.

Brigand A robber.

Goblet A drinking mug.

Holy Land The ancient land of Palestine now divided between Israel and Jordan.

Holy Places Jerusalem and Bethlehem; sacred to Christians and to people of other religions.

Infidels An old name used by Christians for people of a different religion.

Jerkin A jacket.

Lance A knight's spear.

Medieval Anything belonging to or of the time of the Middle Ages (about A.D. 1000-A.D. 1500).

Muslim A follower of Islam.

Pilgrim A person who makes a religious journey to a holy place.

Professional Someone who does something for money or reward.

Saracen The word used by the crusaders to describe all Muslims in the Holy Land.

Shrine A place where a religious leader is remembered.

Traitor A person who betrays his country.

Volunteer To choose to do something.

Vow A religious promise.

INDEX

Picture acknowledgments

The pictures in this book were supplied by the following: BPCC/Aldus Archive (Bodleian Library) 11, 20 (right), 27 (top); BPCC/Aldus Archive 26; Mary Evans Picture Library 13; Ronald Sheridan 27 (bottom), 30. The remaining pictures are from the Wayland Picture Library.